Find an old box,

Lots of cardboard tubes,

Some bright yellow paint

And a little bit of glue.

Build a shining spaceship,
Check for any rust,
Climb up the ladder
And spread some rocket dust.

Zoom past the houses...

Shoot past the stars...

Straight past the moon

And on past Mars!

What's that planet?
No-one ever said
That mud could be blue
And grass could be red!

Oh goodness me!

Whoever is that?

A very strange creature

With a tail like a rat!

"Welcome to Fromble," he said,

Whistling a tune.

"My name is Scrump!

Do you come from the Moon?"

With stars shining brightly,

Fromble Scrump roams.

He finds a special Fromble fruit

So I can take one home.

Wave goodbye to Fromble!

Wave goodbye to Scrump!

Back down to my bedroom,

Landing with a THUMP!

Next time I'll build a rocket

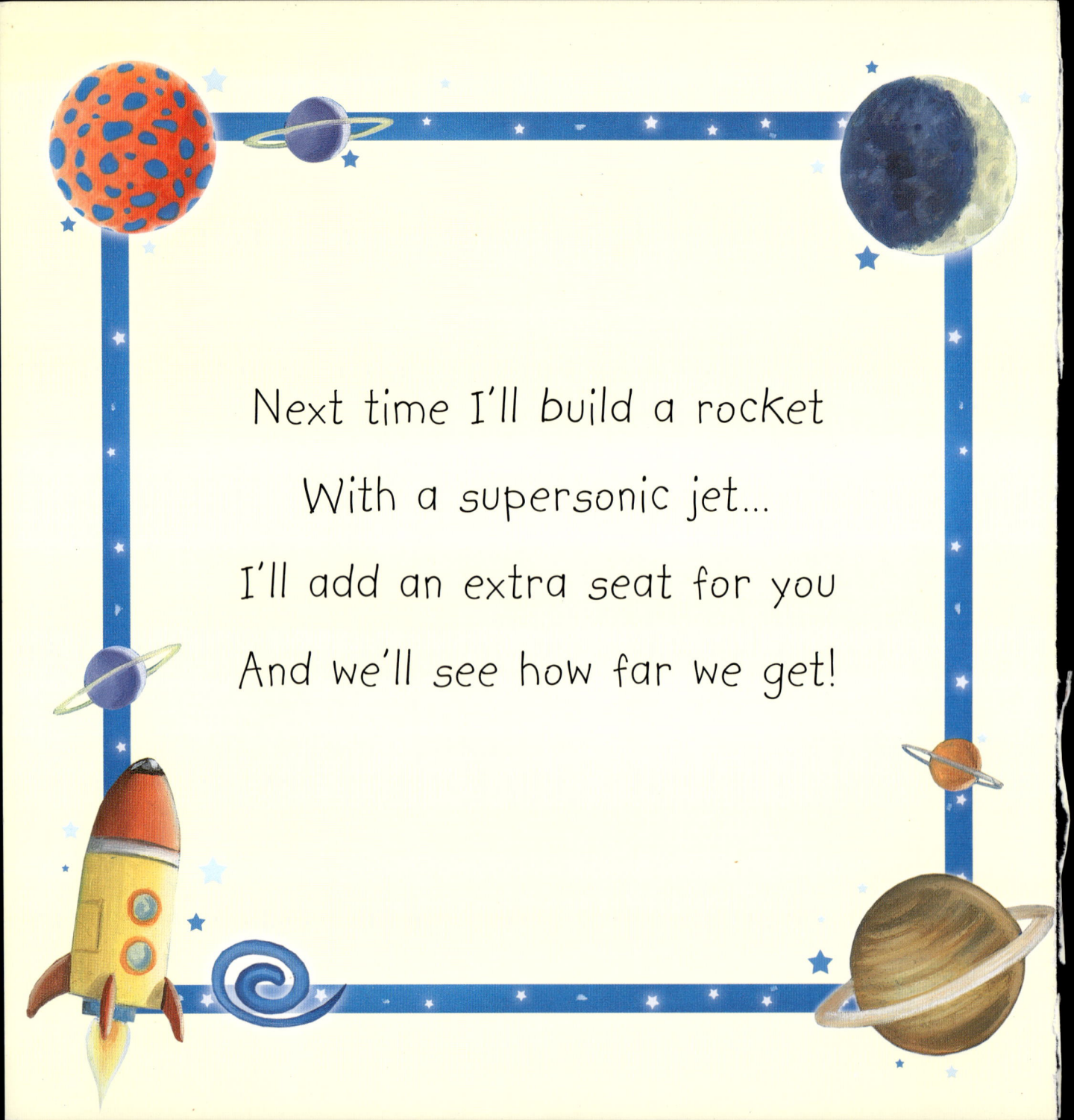

With a supersonic jet...

I'll add an extra seat for you

And we'll see how far we get!